Other Books by Richard Blessing

Poetry

Winter Constellations (Ahsahta, 1977)
A Closed Book (University of Washington, 1981)

Criticism

Wallace Stevens' "Whole Harmonium" (Syracuse, 1970)
Theodore Roethke's Dynamic Vision (Indiana, 1974)

Novel

A Passing Season (Atlantic–Little, Brown, 1982)

Poems & Stories

Richard Blessing

Poems
&
Stories

Dragon Gate, Inc.

Grateful acknowledgment is due to the editors of the
following periodicals, where many of the poems and
stories in the collection were first published: *Poetry
Northwest* ("Late News," "Counting Backward,"
"Callahan Park Field, Bradford, Pennsylvania," "At the
Ballard Locks," "Seizure," "Tumor," "Scott," "Hawk-
Man," "Sundowner" and "Homecoming"); *P-I
Northwest* ("Hospitality," "Grandma and the Eskimos"
and "Learning About the Russians"); *Puget Soundings*
("Teddy Ballgame"); and *Seattle Review* ("A Post-
card"). "At the Ballard Locks" also appeared in *Random
Review 1982.*

The author is grateful to the National Endowment for
the Arts, Literature Program, for a Creative Writing
Fellowship.

9 8 7 6 5 4 3 2
First Printing

Published by DRAGON GATE, INC., 508 Lincoln Street,
Port Townsend, Washington 98368. All rights reserved.

Library of Congress Cataloging in Publication Data

Blessing, Richard Allen.
  Poems & stories.

  I. Title. II. Title: Poems and stories.
PS3552.L44P6   1982   811'.54   82-22177
ISBN 0-937872-12-1
ISBN 0-937872-13-X (paperback)

Contents

Poems & Stories

For the Kid. And for Marlene.

Hospitality

"Uncle Maurice," says the boy, "was my dad as good a swimmer as you?"

"Yuh, Ed was a good swimmer," says Maurice, gazing through the smoke of his Marlboro across the hayfield to the dark shadows of the hemlocks and New England pines. "He swam Silver Lake. I told you that. Remember?"

The boy has rolled the sleeves of his t-shirt up his skinny arms over the shoulder to make them like his uncle's sleeveless undershirt. "But is that far? Was he as good as you?"

"Of course it's far," Maurice says. "It's a lake, ain't it?"

"If my mom doesn't come back," the boy asks, "will I stay with you and Aunt Pauline?"

"She'll come back. Course she'll come back."

A black dog with enormous head and shoulders but almost comically short legs pads up the driveway to the porch. "Old Finnegan," says Maurice. "He's a dandy." The dog flops down between the boy and the heavy-shouldered man, lets his tail rise and fall on the paintless boards.

"I'm hungry," says the boy. "Is it suppertime?"

"Beans is on," says Maurice. "Just waitin' on Pauline now."

"I'm hungry," the boy says again.

"She'll be here," Maurice says. "You can count on her. See that barn shadow? Pretty soon it'll touch the hen house. She'll be here."

"What was my dad like? Was he real big?"

"He was stout in the shoulder and chest. Like you're gonna be. You want to know what he was like, wait till you get growed. Then look in a mirror."

"You think it?"

"I know it," says Maurice, going to the edge of the porch and flipping his cigarette out into the driveway. He squints into the late afternoon sun, takes off his wire-rimmed glasses and cleans them on his undershirt.

"You're getting *fat*," says the boy.

"You think so, MacGregor?" the man chuckles. "Think you're ready to take the old-timer, do ya?" He squares off, narrowing his gray eyes, sniffing loudly, brushing his hawk nose with his right thumb.

Instantly the boy is on him, flailing with his small fists, jumping to reach the chin his uncle thrusts out as a target. "Soft *belly*," says the boy, poking and pummeling the expanse of stomach.

Maurice laughs. "That there's *beer*, MacGregor. Hit that all you want. You break your fist." He frowns. "Hey there, get that thumb outside them fingers. Like this here."

"I wish I could beat up *Carl*," says the boy.

"Your cousin's a little too much for you, bub. I showed him about fighting once my own self."

"Will you teach *me*?"

Maurice is looking up the dusty road to where it bends out of sight against the sky at the top of Derby Hill.

"I said, 'Will you teach me?'"

"It ain't a *how* thing," says Maurice. "It ain't even a *when*."

A crow flies low over the hemlocks, heading for the river. "Pow," says Maurice, pretending to draw down on the bird with a shotgun. "Here comes your aunt."

A dusty black Ford pulls into the driveway. Pauline

12

gets out. Her mouth is very red and she is wearing her fancy shoes with tall heels. The boy has never seen her dressed up. Usually she looks comfortable, like the old kitchen with the wood-burning stove, and all her features fade softly like wallpaper in the parlor. The boy is afraid of the red of her mouth. She might kiss him and it would stick forever.

"You wouldn't believe what happened," she says.

"Um," says his uncle.

A large man is climbing out from behind the wheel. He is a head taller than Maurice. He has a heavy black mustache and a red face.

"'Lo, Maurice," the man says. He does not look at the boy or his uncle.

"First off," says Pauline, "the boat drifted out on the lake. Just broke free. We had to borrow from Chadbin's to hunt *that* down. Then I don't know what all."

"Um," says Maurice again.

"And Charlie here, he just kept sayin', 'We got to be gettin' back. Old Maurice, he'll be thinkin' I don't know what,' and I kept tellin' him he should never mind. 'I know my man,' I told him."

"Stay for supper, Charlie?" asks Maurice. "We got beans on."

"Oh no," says Charlie, waving a big hand. "I couldn't, Maurice."

"C'mon, Charlie," says Pauline. "It's not polite to eat and run." She giggles. "You know Edna's little boy? Name's Mack, but we call him MacGregor."

"Lord yes," says Charlie. He glances at Maurice. "Ain't he growed, though?" He closes the car door. "If you're sure you got enough, then?"

"Plenty," says Maurice. "Plenty."

Finnegan, the old black dog, draws back his lip,

rumbles in his thick throat as Charlie crosses the lawn. The big man hesitates. "Don't worry, Charlie," says Maurice. "Finnegan ain't laid a tooth on a man yet. Course, they's always a first time."

Charlie manages a smile, showing tobacco-stained teeth.

"Come *on*, Charlie," says Pauline.

"Sure," says Maurice. "Come on and feed that gut."

Charlie snorts. "Gut," he says. "You call *this* a gut?" He sticks a tentative finger at Maurice's undershirt front. "Now I ask you, Pauline," he says, "has your old man got a belly here?"

"Belly?" says Maurice, slapping Charlie affectionately on the bicep.

"Belly?" laughs Maurice, cuffing him on the cheek with the other hand.

"Belly?" Maurice says again, backhanding the red-faced man with a sharp popping sound, drawing blood at the corner of the black mustache.

Charlie starts to lift his hands, but Maurice has already driven two hard punches to the face like a man driving nails home. Charlie sits down in the driveway. "Belly?" says Maurice again, putting a heavy boot on Charlie's neck and pushing him down into the gravel.

"Maurice," says Pauline. "Now, honey."

Maurice hooks a boot under Charlie's rump, rolls him over like a dead snake. Then he rolls him over again and again. "Who's got a belly, Charlie?" he says. "Who's got a belly now?"

Charlie mumbles something.

"I don't think Pauline heard you," Maurice says.

"*I* do. I got a belly. Jesus Christ, Maurice."

The boy looks at his aunt. She has wiped the red off her mouth. She is smiling. She leans on the door frame, takes off one tall shoe, then the other. "Maurice," she says, shaking her head. "You, Maurice."

Charlie is sitting in the driveway. Finnegan is barking and snarling at him.

"Well, c'mon in and eat, Charlie," says Maurice. "I wouldn't want you to miss anything me and Pauline has to offer."

"Yes, come on," says Pauline. "I'll feed everybody, man or boy."

Charlie gets up unsteadily and Maurice shoves him gently toward the porch. Pauline laughs. "You, Maurice," she says again.

"Come on, MacGregor," Maurice says to the boy. "You stop that noise now. Charlie and me was just fooling a little. You know how you and Carl fool a little?"

But the boy doesn't move. He stands in the front yard with the black dog, listening to the crow calling from across the river.

His uncle's head looms in the dark of the doorway, his glasses glinting in the last light. "Come on, MacGregor," Maurice says. "Ya gotta eat if you're gonna grow to a man."

And the boy starts slowly up the steps to supper.

Grandma and the Eskimos

"Your Eskimos, now," says my uncle. "In Alaska the Eskimos would handle this thing right."

From another room the voices of women rise and fall like sirens that are far away.

My uncle lifts the lid on the kitchen stove. Flames make shadows play over his angular face. He reaches in the woodbox, lifts out three small birch logs and drops them in the fire. He tosses in the stub of his cigarette, then replaces the lid.

"Yessir," he says, "your Eskimos, they'd handle it right."

My father puffs his pipe and says nothing. He can do this. It's his trick, like weather so nice nobody notices.

"Somebody gets old like that, can't go it, you know," my uncle says, "Eskimos just set her out on the ice. Say good-bye. Go off and don't think about it no more."

A snowy wind drives across my uncle's wide winter fields, rattles the steamy windows of the old farmhouse. It is cozy to be in the dark warm kitchen with the two men, cozy to smell the home-baked bread, the tobacco and beer. The flames rise and fall behind the stove grate.

"What happens then?" I ask.

"Why, there doesn't anything happen," says my uncle. "They just go off is all."

"I sent you to bed an hour ago," says my father, setting down his can of beer. He is not so nice now.

"No," I say. "What happens to the one on the ice?"

"All right," says my father. "No more of that now. Up to bed."

"All right," I say. I get up, and the woman sound is loud, more shrill than wind.

"What's the matter with Grandma?"

"Ain't nothing the matter," my uncle says. "Just women is all."

"Is she crying?"

"Skowhegan," says my father. "That old folks' home. She doesn't want to go."

"Why does she then?"

My uncle goes to the window and looks out at the dark and at the snow coming on and on. He takes down his wool jacket from its peg, the checkerboard one, only green where the red should be, the one with the shoulder patch saying MAINE STATE GUIDE. He pulls it around his shoulders.

"Why does she then?" I say again.

"What can you do?" my father says.

"That's it," says my uncle. "What can a man do?"

"We have to get home to Pennsylvania," says my father. "I have work. Your mother has work. Your Aunt Pauline, she's got the post office."

"I can't be here day 'n night," says my uncle. "What can you do? She can't do nothing for herself."

"Come on," says my father. "I'll get you in bed."

We go out of the warm kitchen into the drafty dining room. The linoleum is cold on my stocking feet. We pass between the mangle and the round oak table and through the parlor where no one ever sits and where I am not allowed to play.

Grandma's room is off the parlor, but the door is closed.

"Come on," says my father. "That's no place for us."

We come to the dark stairs and my father pulls the long string that hangs down from the light at the landing.

A voice behind the closed door, my mother's or my Aunt Pauline's, I can't tell which, says, "Don't say things like that, now, Mama. I can't stand it when you say things like that."

"Things like what?" I ask my father, but he puts a firm hand on my back and starts me up the stairs.

"It's nothing for us," he says.

At the landing we look together out the high window at the white barn and at the snow drifting across the stubbled fields all the way to Chadbin's.

"I bet it's cold," I say. "Carl and Clair, did you know, when they have to go to the bathroom, they have to walk outside?"

"Sure," says my father. "What did you think?"

"I'm glad we don't."

"Indoor plumbing," my father says. "Noblest advance of civilized man."

I like the old high-ceilinged bedroom with the big white bed, wide enough for two grownups, where I sleep by myself. I like the picture of my aunt and my mother in the wooden oval frame where they stare out all night like two serious dolls.

Wind shakes the house. I pull the quilted comforter up to my nose and pretend there are wolves. I am sinking down into the feathery mattress. My father sits beside me on the bed.

"Is Mama crying?"

"Hush," says my father. "Maybe a little. Go to sleep."

"I can't. Tell me a story."

"No. Tomorrow's a long, long day."

"Tell me about the Eskimos."

"Eskimos? I don't know that. That's Alaska."

"What about the one on the ice? Uncle Maurice says they go off and don't think about it again."

18

"I don't know."

"He wouldn't lie."

"No."

"Does the one on the ice just get a cold and die?"

My father, who almost never touches me, brushes back my hair.

"It's going to sleep, is all," says my father. "And then dreams."

"What does he dream, the one on the ice?"

"I don't know. An Eskimo dream."

"What?"

"Lots of things. Maybe about killing his first seal or a white bear he saw once on an ice cake. Maybe how the snow was the morning his little boy was born."

"Good dreams?"

"Sure," says my father, getting up to go downstairs. He is tall in the doorway, and strong-looking.

"That's good."

"Sure."

From downstairs the sound of the women rises up and I think again about wolves circling in the dark fields outside.

"Daddy," I say, "I never want to be old."

"Hush," says my father. "It's all right. Really, it's all right."

"I'm never going to be," I say.

"Kid," says my father, "it's the best there is."

Learning About the Russians

"The trouble," I tell my uncle, "is you don't know history, political science, or economics."

"The trouble," my uncle says, "is you don't know squat."

The trouble, probably, is we are both right. It is past midnight in the warm, high-ceilinged kitchen of the old farmhouse, and we are talking politics.

"What don't I know?"

"The world," says my uncle. "College ain't the world. You wasn't in a war. And you don't know the Rooshians."

"The Russians?"

"That's right," says my uncle. "That dark-hair fella what had the dog? Needed a shave? Right hand to the bald general?"

"Nixon?" I say.

"Yeah, him," my uncle says. "Now he understood your Rooshians. He knew the world."

My aunt, almost exactly between us in age, hates politics and wishes we'd stop. She yawns theatrically. "Maurice," she says. "Maurice, I have to be at the post office tomorrow."

"Well, go on to bed then," he says. "Ain't nobody keeping you."

The phone rings, stopping us all.

"That'll be Mama," says my aunt. "She's gone. I know it."

"No such thing," says my uncle, picking up the receiver.

"Yeah, Micky," he says. My aunt sighs, sinks down

into a chair.

"No," says my uncle. "We was just turnin' in, anyway. Don't mind that."

Then, "Yeah, I know Eddie." He listens. "Yeah, him and Lena been havin' some troubles." He listens again, and the voice on the other end rises. "How many?" says my uncle. And then, "You think just the one?"

He takes down the khaki shirt from the peg behind the stove, the one with the dark brown patch saying SHER-IFF PENOBSCOT COUNTY, and fishes an arm through a sleeve.

"Okay, Micky," he says. "I'll have a run out." There is another pause. "No. Don't need no help. I know Eddie. Much obliged all the same."

He hangs up and turns to us. He is still a handsome man, the face lean and hawklike under the thatch of gray hair. Next month he will be sixty-five.

"Micky Dugan," he says. "Eddie Youngblood and Lena been kicking up a bit. I'll make a little run out there."

"Those Indians," says my aunt.

"I know Eddie," says my uncle. "He's all right."

He finishes putting on the shirt. Then he goes to the locked cabinet in his little room off the parlor and unlocks it and takes out the police .38 and the heavy deer rifle, the Savage.

"No," says my aunt.

"Where's my damn badge?" says my uncle, sitting down heavily and pulling on his boots.

"Where you left it, most likely," says my aunt. She is twisting and untwisting a dish towel. "Just the one what?"

My uncle looks blank.

"On the phone with Micky," she says. "You asked how many and you said just the one."

"Did I?" says my uncle. "I don't remember."

"Mack," my aunt says to me, "you go with him."

"No," says my uncle.

"Maurice," she says, "you're sixty-five. Look at the size of him. You'll be the death of me."

"I'd like to go," I say.

"No," he says.

"Hey," I say. "I leap tall buildings at a single bound. I'm for truth, justice and the American way. I'd like to go."

"Please, Maurice," says my aunt.

"All right," says my uncle. "But you keep your trap shut, and you do what you're told."

In the Land Rover he puts the Savage in the gunrack, finds he's forgotten the keys. He sends me back for them, and then we go lurching out of the gravel driveway and head west, toward Milo.

"Where we going?"

"Indian Pond," he says. "Now the situation's this. Micky Dugan lives uproad of Eddie Youngblood. Says Eddie and his wife been makin' a racket, yellin' and such like. But somebody fired a shot, and Micky, he don't want to be the one to find out who."

"A shot? Is he sure?"

"Micky's lived here all his life. He knows a shot."

We're driving through Milo now. Maurice never pays attention to stop signs, blasts on through, spraying gravel on the lawns, all dandelion and tall grass by day, flashes past the gabled New England houses and the Dairy Queen, and then on northeast out of town.

"Keep a watch out for deer," he says. "Now," he says, "the reason why I brought you along is this. They ain't gonna be no trouble. I know Eddie. He's a good man, fought in the big war. But if they is trouble, I want you to drive this here Land Rover back over to Derby, pick up Craig and Bob and Bucky. You got it?"

"Why don't we get them on the way?"

"Kee-rist," says my uncle, swerving hard left to miss a deer, a young doe, that suddenly shoots across our headlights. "Keep a watch!"

A mile later I ask again. "Why not get Craig and them now?"

"Because they ain't gonna be no trouble. You don't wake a man up what's got work in the mornin'. Only if they is trouble, I'm saying."

He turns hard off the main road, sliding on the dirt of the Indian Pond road.

"Damn," he says. "Time was, a man walked three, four hours to get to water here. Now every city slicker with the price of gas can drive his boat right on in. Might's well put in damn parkin' meters, is what they might's well."

The road is bumpy, high-crowned with grasses and big rocks. We pass cabins every hundred yards or so, all of them dark. The trees close in over the road, big hemlocks and maples mostly. My uncle slows the Land Rover.

"I'm gonna turn off the lights," he says. "This next quarter mile is gonna be a rough one, so keep a watch out." He begins inching along the road, driving with his head out the window. "When I get out," he says, "you get out on my side. Keep the Land Rover between you and the camp."

He coasts in and stops. I can hear the lake washing up on the rocks through the trees. The peepers are loud. I can hear my heart. My uncle slides out of the Land Rover and I follow him awkwardly, tangling my feet in the brake and clutch. I slide loudly to one knee beside him. Over the hood, about twenty yards from the road, I can see the dim outline of a small trailer on cement blocks. Nothing moves.

"Eddie," my uncle yells. "Eddie Youngblood?" The peepers stop and begin again. His voice echoes from the rocks, from the stand of dark hemlock and pine behind the trailer house.

"Eddie? This here's Maurice Shreve."

I start to stand up, but my uncle grabs my belt and pulls me back into a half-crouch.

Then a voice, almost a howl, comes out of the dark trailer. "White man, go away. This is nothing for you, white man."

"Come on now, Eddie," shouts my uncle. "This is Maurice. We was on the same side in the big war, wasn't we? They wasn't no white man, no Indian, to it."

"Maurice," comes the voice. Echoes make me think it's behind me. "You go away. I'll tend to it."

"What have you done, Eddie?"

No answer.

"Where's little Nancy?"

"She's at her grandmother's. Just at her grandma's is all."

"Lena?"

Again there is no answer, only a soft sound like an owl might make, or a man, crying.

"Let me talk to Lena, Eddie. If I can talk to Lena, I'll go away."

"Do you want the gun?" I whisper.

He silences me with a quick gesture of his hand. I can see more now. Moonlight falls on the trailer through the trees.

"Maurice? You get out of here, now. I'm gonna start shooting."

"Come on, now, Eddie. I got my new Land Rover out here. I got my nephew from college out here. You don't want to shoot up my new rig, do you?"

"Will he shoot?" I say.

"Maybe she ain't dead, Eddie," my uncle shouts, ignoring me. "Maybe we can save her yet if you'll let me help."

"It's no good, Maurice," says the voice from the trailer. "I shot her face away. They ain't nothin' there."

"Well Eddie," says my uncle, "you'll just have to do the right thing now."

"They was other men, Maurice. White men, too."

"Well, that's hard," says my uncle. "But it will all look different tomorrow."

"Her face is terrible." The peepers go on with their business. The lake scuffs in against the shore three times, four. "Worse than the war, Maurice."

"Ain't nothin' you can do now, Eddie. You just have to be a soldier. You was a good soldier, remember?"

My uncle hands me the Land Rover keys.

"The bastards wouldn't leave her alone, she was so pretty, Maurice," Eddie shouts. "And now her face . . ."

There is no more sound from the trailer except for the owl-like whisper.

My uncle stands up slowly. He loosens his .38 in the leather holster, gestures to me to stay where I am. He steps around the Land Rover and stands in the Youngblood yard, knee-deep in fern.

"I'm gonna come on in now, Eddie," he says. There is no answer. The peepers make a constant shrill, like the sound in my ears. Fireflies appear and disappear in the grass of the road crown.

My uncle makes his way across the yard, not hurrying, like a man paying a call. When he steps on the cement block that serves both as porch and doorstep, he says something, very soft, that I can't hear. Then he pulls open the door and stands to one side. Over the peepers, over the sound of the lake, I hear a metallic click. Even a city slicker knows what it is.

My uncle murmurs something again, so faint it is like wind in the trees. Then he steps through the door. Moonlight catches his khaki shirt and then he's gone. I slip into the driver's seat, fit the key into the ignition, try to remember where reverse is on the Land Rover.

And then they come out, Youngblood first, then my uncle, carrying a rifle in the crook of his arm.

"Eddie," says my uncle, "I don't guess you know Mack. Pauline's sister's boy, you know?"

Eddie is nearly my uncle's age, a short man with black hair and a flat face on which horn-rimmed glasses are the most striking feature. He wipes his hand across his pudgy belly where the t-shirt almost reaches his trousers. "Glad ta meetcha," he says, and I take his hand. It is warm and a little sticky. I don't know what to say, so I just nod.

"Better you sit in back," my uncle says to me. By the quick inside light as the door opens and closes, I see the faint trace of blood on my palm. My uncle hands the rifle in to me, and I notice he has taken out the clip and put it in his shirt pocket. Then he hands back the Savage. Eddie gets in front in the passenger seat and my uncle slides in behind the wheel. He starts the engine, turns on the lights. The eyes of some animal, quite large, flash in the trees.

"Deer," says Maurice.

"They's a lot of 'em back in here," says Eddie.

My uncle turns into the yard of the trailer, then backs out onto the road.

"Will she be all right?" Eddie asks.

"Sure," says Maurice. "Won't nobody bother her. Take care of it first thing in the morning."

Eddie starts to cry then, his whole body shaking. My

26

uncle waits, leaning on the wheel, staring straight ahead up the road. The Land Rover idles quietly.

After a while the crying stops, but the body goes on shivering. "Christ, Maurice," he says. "You and me. Carl Chadbin. Wayne Smallbear. When the Rooshians come, we was going to take to the woods. Live off the land, remember? Fish and hunt, like the old times. They wouldn't nobody find us."

"The Rooshians ain't comin', Eddie. That game's up for all of us."

"She was so pretty, Maurice," Eddie says. "And now, her face, you know. There's nothin' there."

My uncle puts a hand on Eddie's shoulder. "We'll fix her up," he says. "Don't think about it now."

"There's nothin' left to fix."

"Don't think about it," says my uncle. "That Wilber Clay now, over to Milo? He's a whiz. I seen men come in there so stove up—a lot worse than this here. And Wilber, he has 'em lookin' good as ever before."

"You think it?"

"Sure."

"That'd be good. Her mama then, and Nancy. They could pay last respects."

"Sure," says my uncle, putting the Land Rover in gear and starting up the camp road toward the highway. "And they'll put her in Evergreen there. With them big trees and all. The Penobscot running down below."

"You think?"

"Sure. We'll just drive over to Milo now. See the magistrate."

"Christ, Maurice. She was too pretty."

"Don't think about it," says my uncle. "It's no good thinking about it now."

Late News

In a small town in western Pennsylvania, a Polish workman
is killing everyone.

                          Who can say how the world seems
to Dombrowski this morning? It is as different
as a Doberman's or a general's.

                          If this is a war,
Dombrowski is winning. If we are the enemy,
as by now we are, cover his hairy chest with ribbons.

Dombrowski peers out of his shell of a house
and the neighbors go round like neighbors
in a gallery and the police go round.

A man down the line at the plant says *Things*
ate on him lately, but no more than nobody else.
He does not wish to be named.

                          The dead
do not wish to be named, pending notification.

It is a quiet neighborhood, the kids lying
beside their bicycles, the lovers kissing nothing
forever on the porch swing.

                          Is there something
Dombrowski wants? The chief says *A nut like that,*

they ought to kill themself.

What if, in sullen wisdom,
we give in, retreat from the little town, or all
of Pennsylvania? Let the mad inherit their corner
of earth.

There would be space for miles
where only wind would blow. After a while, the mines
would go back to the grass. Bass would lie deep
in the Allegheny, as if they had never gone away.

One morning even Dombrowski might lay down his gun,
walk naked in a meadow that had been his yard.
Great waves of butterflies would ride the wind
and the ground would drum with distant hooves.

There is a sun so old no man has seen it.
In Pennsylvania, Dombrowski lifts his eyes.

State of Women

Seattle. Three men are beating a woman
with a rubber-coated pipe because parking
is scarce in the city, like a cop
when you need one.

                   In the courthouse square
three quieter men are sitting on a woman
to take off her rings.

              What's going on?

If women didn't fuck, says Senator Tower,
straight from the crotch, *there'd be a bounty*.
The old boys nod in their hallowed network.
There ought to be a law.

                  A salesman I know,
before he left, broke his wife's jaw.
She wanted to be equal, so I hit her
like a man.

          Senator, it's season enough
for men to go away a spell, to take some smoky
Eastern state and throw the women out.

Let there be two cars for every parking space

and alleys dark enough to redistribute wealth.
Legislate no rubber coating on the pipes.

Whatever hulks out in twenty blood-dimmed years
will be no slouch, wading the shallow river
to some milder state.

                    Cornflowers
dazzle his hungry eyes for miles
and quail hens whistle under berry vines.

He arrives, like a forgotten anniversary,
at a village, modest sun-colored cottages
with heavy orchards and arbors with grapes.
It is evening.

              How calmly they rise, a formation
of athletes, hair falling light and dark
as clouds. What will become of him,
the breastless stranger, shaking a battered fist,
crying *You need me* in the old language
no one, no one knows.

Counting Backward

Each night my father counts backward from 100 like a shepherd
climbing down meadow by meadow the Alps.

                              Since his stroke
he does this, he says, so his mind holds still, so it freezes,
a suspect, hands on the wallpaper. That way it is there
with his cane the next morning.

                         When your mind runs away,
well, it stashes parts of your real life forever, the names
of lakes, the pretty faces of girls.

                         When that happens,
you count on nothing, a patch of sun on a green carpet,
new snow on a roof framed by curtains. You call the woman
"Nurse" and wonder why she cries.

                              It is still a life,
that chair between the cashews and windows.

                              Then one day
Bang! Doesn't your mind come waltzing home, made up
clown-style, sloshing memories like confetti in a pail?
And don't you take your life in your hands, counting
out good times, counting out bad, marking time
backward so it's understood?

                    Whatever you're missing,

he says, *it's what you don't miss.*

Listen, he says,
that sound in the old high ceilings of the house,
not ice in the eaves, no man's voice, no echo either . . .

Only the wind, counting toward zero.

Callahan Park Field, Bradford, Pennsylvania

Mid-August.

            My father, who is old enough to play dead,
takes the mound instead. He leaves his cane like a bat
in the dugout rack.

             Under this sky familiar as wallpaper
in an old bedroom, the scent of fresh-mowed grass
filling the air like applause, with a glove older
than I am, he is coming back.

             How they conspire
against me, father and son, put me out to pasture,
my middle-aged back against the wall in deepest left
where the flagpole flies no flag this bright blue day
except fall wind bannering the end of a season.

My side retired, this is their series, their world,
my son with a boy's voice and a man's shoulders,
my iron-man father, who used to throw smoke.

                                Now
his arm rises heavily, like the rusted donkey pumps
still working the crude hills behind me
in these played-out fields, and falls.

And my boy, his red hair blazing like a sun

going down, is swinging, swinging from the heels.
Only connect is the thing, and he does.

                             It may be
that our blood fails. But the ball leaps in a long arc.
My God, it is making the field small, and here,
across the field, across the years, comes the sound
of bat on ball, sweet as any tea cake, connecting us all.

Remember the man in Pittsburgh, how he used to call it?
Open the window, Aunt Minnie, here she comes!
Remember Mel Allen? *Going . . . going . . . GONE!*

At the Ballard Locks

Midsummer.

We stand at the rail, stiff and dumb as pilings,
linked by the ropes of one another's arms.
The salmon are running.

                       Freshwater madness
is in them and they leap like sparks
from some windy chimney. It is only
that they have come so far.

Or is it that they remind us of characters
from that old movie, lovers who age
like apples on a sunny windowsill, falling
in on themselves, dying at the end
believing nothing dies?

                    It is only that they
remind us of ourselves, sprung jaw and raw tail,
egg white for an eye, or torn, worthless fin.

Is there in nature or out of nature or half in
and out as here in this man-made channel
locking fresh water to the sea, these
salmon ladders of poured cement, gawkers
at every porthole, no song but this one
of self-mourning?

                  They do not mourn. They do not seem

to mourn. See, there and there another one
rises out of the narrowed sea his shining
body's length and higher.
                              They split the heart
of the sun going down.

                              Not feeding, someone
says along the rail. *They've come too far
for that.*

              Still, they fling their lives
in violent, graceful gestures,
four and five a minute, falling with a smack
flat as a butcher's palm.

                              I remember
on your birthday you were sad. *I won't be
rich or famous*, you said. *And I don't have
a baby. Now it's too late.*

                              Never too late,
the sea thrashes out and in. Look.
How purely it is sex and death.
I pull you close. We have missed nothing.
It is our only life.

A Postcard

"Greetings from Beaufort, NC," it says, "known for Southern hospitality, colonial architecture, sea oaks, fishing, sailing and quaint old churches. In one of these we were married today. It was a surprise to all."

"Your mother is married," I say to the boy, who is playing a complicated baseball game with dice on the floor.

"To John?" he asks.

"She doesn't say. Knowing her—" I break off. "Yeah. Sure. To John."

He rolls the dice, bends to the game board.

"Does it bother you?" Caitlin asks. She is watching me closely.

"It's the weather from Raleigh-Durham," I say.

"Are you sure?"

"Sure."

"Don't worry," says the boy. "You're still my dad." He rolls the dice again, records a hit or an out. "Aren't you?"

"Of course he is," says Caitlin. "Who else would have you?"

"I remember Beaufort," I say. "When you were little your mother and I walked through the cemetery there."

"It does bother you," says Caitlin. "I know it. It's all right. You should just say so."

"When they get back, who will I stay with?" the boy asks.

"It doesn't bother me," I say, "but I liked Beaufort."

"We should go there," Caitlin says. "She's not the only

43

one who can get married."

"Me too?" the kid wants to know.

"Of course you too," says Caitlin. "What kind of wedding would it be without the children?"

"You could hear the sea anywhere in Beaufort," I say. "They have the smallest police station you ever saw, practically a phone booth."

"Really," says Caitlin. "It's all right."

"A *phone* booth?" the boy says.

Out the window, down two stories, the maintenance man is painting white lines on the parking lot. Beyond the lot, the dumpster, beyond the torn-up patch of ground with the odd ends of building materials still to be picked up, they have begun to bulldoze the woods.

"We loved the cemetery. It would really be something. I mean, in winter, when the tourists went home. Listening to the waves. All the oaks have moss hanging. The houses are white all the way to the sea."

"Do we have to talk about it?" Caitlin asks.

The boy goes on rolling the dice. He mutters to himself, bends to his scorepad.

"Listen, there was a man there, a sailor. They buried him standing up!"

"Why'd they do that?" The boy folds his game away.

"And all the babies. Maybe twenty babies, not even two years old, from diphtheria in just one winter. And later the kids—fifteen, sixteen—in the Civil War. The place was full of carved stone lambs, and under the stone lambs these—babies."

"Why did they?"

"What?"

"Bury him that way? Standing up?"

Caitlin stands at the window. The sun is the color of her long hair. "Damn them!" she says. "See what they're

44

doing to the trees!''

"I forget," I say. "He was a British sailor. The other side. Maybe he has to stand up always for being wrong."

"That's *morbid*," Caitlin says. "The dead are *dead*."

"Except for ghosts," says the boy. "Then they aren't."

Across the field the summer leaves rise and fall. The bulldozer roars and subsides, builds again and again.

"No," I say. "*I'm* wrong. It wasn't punishment. He asked for it."

"Why did he?"

The boy is at the window, leaning against Caitlin. Her arm rests across his shoulders. Soon he will be as tall as she is.

"Perpetual salute. He asked to be buried at attention, facing England, facing his King. I think that's right."

"I think that's nuts," the boy says. "How would the King know?"

"He *wouldn't* know," says Caitlin, giving the kid a squeeze. "And he wouldn't care either."

"He's still at attention," I say. "It doesn't matter what the King knows, what the Queen cares. It's the sailor."

"Yes," she says. "You and the sailor."

"It's only a story," I say. "You don't have to do that. Don't do that, now. It's only a story."

"I guess you had to be there," Caitlin says.

Teddy Ballgame

It's my weekend, so we go to the ballgame.

"Did you ever see that guy play, you know, that Mr. Coffee guy?" the boy asks.

"DiMaggio? No," I say, "but I saw Teddy Ballgame, Ted Williams."

"Was he great? How many times?"

"Just once. It wasn't like this, drive ten minutes to the dome, park, and walk in. It was 200 miles to Cleveland, five hours. If it rained when you got there, you turned around and drove home."

"How old were you?"

"Ten. Eleven maybe. A little younger than you."

"Did your dad take *you*?"

"Yeah. It was a surprise. He knew I loved Ted Williams."

"That was nice," the boy says. We come to a stoplight at the corner of Dearborn, the Kingdome looming now at the end of the street.

"He was like that. He didn't have much money. We had the worst seats. But you could see home plate."

"And Ted Williams."

"Yes," I say. "And Ted Williams." We're back in traffic, squinting into the sun that falls in long skeins across the Sound from the Olympics.

"What was so great? I mean what did he do?"

"It was a doubleheader. He was one for ten, a home run."

"One for *ten*? That's not so hot!"

"In the middle of the second game—he was about

nothing for eight then—he missed a pitch and stepped out. I remember he put the bat between his legs, scooped some dirt, and rubbed his hands together like he had the pitcher's neck in there. A man behind us said, 'There's a home run on those hands right now!'"

"Was there?"

"He struck out."

The boy laughs. "But the next time," I go on, "the next time against The Bear Garcia he hit it out."

"Was it far?"

"I suppose it gets farther every year. I remember it was high. I remember it against the sky above the rim of Cleveland Stadium. It couldn't have been, but that's what I remember. And that he didn't swing hard, everything came together smooth and easy."

"Who won?"

"Cleveland I think. I don't remember."

"You're funny, what you remember," the boy says as we turn into the parking lot. I pay the attendant and we start walking.

"Did he hit it farther than we saw Oscar Gamble hit it?"

"Probably not. But it was different. He was Ted Williams. The grass was real. Your Grandpa said, 'There. That's something. You have that now!'"

"Did he really say that, or is that just what you remember?"

"It doesn't matter. Something like that. 'Now you've seen something. You have that!'"

The crowd thickens near the turnstiles. The scorebook, the pennant vendors, are working us all. I buy a scorebook, hand it to the boy.

"Did Grandma go to the game?"

"Sometimes. Not that one. She didn't like baseball."

We pass through the turnstiles, start up the ramp. It is cool under the dome. A cave, a stone house.

"My mom does. She likes baseball."

"She does. I know she does," I say. "She used to play right field for the law school softball team. The only woman."

"Could she go with us sometimes?"

"I don't know, kid. Maybe sometime. I don't know."

We catch our first glimpse of the playing field. It's impressive, the vast green carpet under the arching vault of grayish stone.

"Well," he says, "I have Oscar Gamble. That's something too."

"Yes," I say. "It's what it is. I just wish it could be Ted Williams."

"Ruppert Jones," he says. "Bruce Bochte."

"Ballplayers," I say. "This is the big leagues, and they're here."

The National Anthem. The Mariners freeze at attention, small figures in their home whites, blue trim. The final notes echo from the stone sky. Play ball! Play ball!

"Dad," my boy says, "I'm glad we came."

Song on Royal Street

"Ahh, go buy yourself a set of legs," he snarls at the chubby black dachshund that waddles after them, barking.

"Willow Street, remember?" she says. "Could it be the same dog?"

"After thirteen years? And this one almost a puppy?"

"All right, then," she says. "It's the puppy of the same one."

They are walking the streets of New Orleans, the University district, on a night heavy with rain-like mist. The dog stops to sniff the trunk of a mimosa, and they walk on under the broad-leaved trees. The scent of honeysuckle is everywhere.

"Old age," he says. "Ain't it great?"

"Come on," she says. "Forty isn't old age."

He is conscious of added weight at the middle, flesh under the jawline. He thinks how well she has aged. The blonde hair is curled now, short and becoming, and the body is fuller, a woman's body and not a girl's.

"It's just nothing is like we planned," he says. "Like I planned."

"Nothing ever is. For anybody. But has it been *so* bad?"

Tulane Stadium rises out of the mist like a cathedral in some history book, dwarfing the houses for blocks around.

"Not for you, maybe," he says. "You have the boy."

"Look," she says. "The stadium. Remember that Thanksgiving in the French Quarter motel and then we came up here for the game?"

"I remember. Tulane lost."

"I don't remember the game."

"Ah," he says, "thank you for that."

For a moment they drift together, shoulders touching. "I miss this city," he says.

"It's not so bad," she says. "We have a happy kid, a healthy one."

"*You* have."

"Don't say that," she says. "He misses you, he does, but he understands."

Crickets chirr in the dark grass. Her heels are lower these days, he notices. Sensible shoes make her seem smaller, diminished. She barely reaches his shoulder.

"Do you believe in magic?" he asks. "There was that old Negro woman on Royal Street, oh way back, when we were just beginning. She wanted money. Remember?"

"No."

"She wanted money and I walked away. You must remember. She came up behind us then and took my hand and she sang something. You remember."

"No."

"And after, I had to sit down, I felt that sick and dizzy. You said it was nerves. You said it was not eating. You said I was making it up. Imagining things."

"I don't remember."

"After that we were never happy."

"I don't remember."

"All right," he says, "all right. Anyway, we have a healthy kid."

"That's a lot."

"That's something."

"Yes."

They turn up McAlister Drive, passing the brick dormitories, the broad shadowed quadrangles. It is late summer. The students have all gone home. He bends his head passing under the mimosas, the low-hanging boughs.

"Was there really a black woman?" she asks.

"I had to sit down, I was that sick. And the next day we found out you were pregnant. Remember now? And then things just happened like they happened. She sang a song on Royal Street."

"I remember you were scared. Like a boy. I remember you wanted the baby dead."

"No."

"'There are ways,' you said. 'I know people,' you said."

"No. The Negro woman. She sang a song and I got sick."

"You wanted him dead. I don't remember a woman."

They have come to a corner, the streetlamps glimmering through the heavy leaves of trees. A bus flashes past and disappears into mist and dark.

"Look," he says, "the Freret Jet. We rode that enough times. Boy, the Freret Jet. I remember that."

"I think you made that up," she says. "About the black woman."

"After she sang, you never made it," he says. "Not one time."

"I was morning sick."

"Not one time."

"She didn't take *my* hand. She never sang to *me*."

"You remember then?"

"No."

He drives his fist against a stop sign and sinks to one knee in pain. He looks up at her. "There was a woman," he says slowly. "She took my hand. On Royal Street. She sang a song."

"She never took my hand."

"It was never any good again. Not once."

"I was sick with Chris. And then Daddy died."

"Lots of people die."

"Not like that. Not so horribly."

"But never again."

"Not never," she says. "Just never for you."

"Liar," he says. "Never again in your life."

She turns to him then and her eyes burn through the mist. "All right," she says, "all right. I remember the woman. She was horrible, all wrinkles and bad smell. When she took your hand her eyes shone red in the dark like a swamp animal."

"No," he says. "She was just an old beggar."

"When she crooned, there was death in her voice. She made you a dead man, and you didn't know."

"I don't remember."

"You remember, all right. After that, touching you was a nightmare. You stunk of the grave, a dead man walking around. Look at you. You're more dead than my father."

"There was never a woman. Or not like that. I made her up, an excuse."

"No. After that I never came with you. Remember?"

"No."

"She was old and horrible and you wouldn't give her money. She touched you with her putrefying hand. She put a spell on you on Royal Street. I never made it again, not with you. Everyone else. Never with you."

"I made her up."

"No. Stop crying."

"I can't. I don't have anything, not even my boy."

"Stop crying."

"You never came, not once."

"You were afraid."

"Not once."

"When I touched you," she says, "I was touching death."

He sits down on the cold stone of the gymnasium stairs. She moves in and out of focus, like someone seen through poorly adjusted binoculars.

"The black woman," he says.

"Yes," she says, "the black woman."

"No," he says. "It was your hand, your song."

"All right," she says, "all right. We have a fine son."

"Yes," he says. "That's a lot. That's everything."

"He isn't even yours," she says.

Seizure

for Rick Rapport

It's the pulsing engine pulling cars in a train.
After it, a name, effect, cause, then meaning
and meaning rattling to the end, the brakeman
waving good-bye.

              Life is like that:
lived forward, we understand it backward,
and too late.

            Arrested by lawful authority,
the dictionary says. *Also, an apprehension.*

It's when your left hand, clenched and cold,
distant as the moon, shoots itself crazy
at the wrong goal, at the hanging net.
It's when you are thrown on the unmerciful court
you have always loved, the man defending you
justly crying *Foul*.

              You are guilty and charged,
completely a jerk, a layman contesting the law
of motion. Brainless, your hand shakes up,
an eager sophomore in a college of hard knocking.

In a different sense, it's a title. And after,
a poem, dreadful with puns.

                It is beginning
wisdom, an apprehension of Law.

Subtraction

> A mathematical process in which one
> number or quantity is deducted from
> another and which can be generalized
> by the formula $m - s = r$ in which
> the remainder r when added to the
> subtrahend s always reproduces the
> minuend m.

To reduce generalization, think of yourself as minuend.
The result is negative.

And label *Obsolete* this definition:
Withdrawing a right to which one is entitled. The way
things are, you are entitled to nothing, save your opinion,
which you may count all you like. It adds little
to the answer, which is otherwise right.

Additionally, your case (which is mine for the moment)
is not a problem of rights, but lefts—left arm
and left leg, the subtrahends, remaining, reproducing
nothing equal to the quantity of numbers done,
uncalculated, a month ago.

Always a fast glove man,
you can't get to third base now, your left leg
wandering imperceptibly off its line. Shiftless
and driven by turns, you still make payments
on your worthless car.

Let the brainy surgeons,
k and r, calculate risks for b, who stands here
uncertainly for you, for me, for all those lessened

in the sciences of loss. Let them do little harm,
or none.

Our birth sign is the subtraction mark.
Was it Thales or Kierkegaard, the only wise men
watered down enough, who said, *Only the broken self
becomes a self*?

Tumor

for Lisa Arrivey

Like proud grandparents cornering a reluctant stranger,
they show me the pictures, pin them up, backlighting.
Left lobe and right, major and minor hemispheres,
they are walnuts, just as the textbooks say.
Let no poet improve on *that*.

                              And the left lobe,
my right hand, my noble and ignoble speech, sweet reason,
is whiter than the snow that surprised us last night
and which hangs still on the roofs of the modest houses
across the street.

                    Ah, but the right! Blacker
than a coal miner's lung or a house new to mourning!
Is this what comes of them, my evil fantasies,
the sexual one guarded years like a microdot, my greed,
my pettiness, my unambiguous pleasure in a colleague's
bad reviews? Or is it only that, after all,
it has to be *someone*, has always been someone,
no trick to it really, no cause nor effect,
but always someone else. Today I am someone.

Take courage from this: it is not so bad as you think
it would be when you imagine it. I wouldn't lie to you.

It is only the minor hemisphere. All the things
I was never good for: singing and music, spatial relations,
the left-hand lay-in, the occult crafts and arts.
Always my tin ear, the one for listening when a bush

bursts suddenly into flame or when a whirlwind
has something it wants to say.

                         It is only
the minor hemisphere; that, and the fear on the faces
of friends, remembering I was young and more handsome
than any Phoenician, killing themselves being kind.

I set this down like a farmer planting at the bitterest end
of winter, perhaps before. I watch the sky. One way
or another, I will outlive this all.

Hawk-Man

for Dana Powell

Wheeling and wheeling in the widened corridors,
the hawk-man listens for the wind. Buckle-high,
hour by round hour, his fire eye burns down.

And his circle has no end: nurses' station
and treatment room, the jigsawed patients' lounge,
the numbered doorways. Once more the elevators,
uplifting outsiders, visitors in a snake-and-bird house,
wanting to be somewhere else.

                      Wanting to be somewhere else,
I ask a nurse, the heartbreaker, farm girl from Omaha.
Hang gliding, she says, like naming a disease.

For a week I watch him, a beard red and burnished
as hot blood, the fever eye, the hands crooked
like meat-hooks on the wheels. His shadow
crosses my sleep in a long barnyard dream.

Meanwhile, doctors scribble letters in my palms
like prescriptions, asking *What do you feel?*
What do you feel now?

                It is hard to say.
Right now I feel I am the lucky one. It may be
I misread the letters. Everything

is upside down, or backwards.

                                    When I am stronger,
I walk beside him in the halls. Lacking weather,
we are talking about will, the human will.

One thing about it, he says, *your neurology
just don't give a shit!* I follow him, drawn up,
far as I dare, high enough so every landmark
shrinks and spins.

                          What's hard, he says,
they never fucking tell you yes or no.
When I can, I ask the nurse, my Omaha girl.
They tell him, she says. *He just won't hear.*

Scott

for Eileen Cody

Spinning his wheels, up against the wall, he can't stand
for us all. Still, he's not far from me, or even you,
only an eye-blink from the man in the street.

When she has time the nurse, too tall for marriages
she says, peels him from the wall he's climbing,
gives him a send-off. Feeling no pain, he rolls
his life, two years or twenty, depending what you count,
up-corridor, erratic as a top just before the fall.

Now the joyride, that dead friend who drove him,
are more lost to him than the combination
to your high school locker, or that everyday walk
to the lot where you park.

Scott's my baby,
says the nurse. In two months she has taught him
to feed himself, and he does, like a wild joker,
face on the table.

What a piece of work this man,
cut more places than a marked deck, more broken
than a windshield, stitched into misshapes
even a mother can love.

One rule, says the nurse,
vowels flat as Nebraska. *Don't* you *go helping.*
My ward, you learn to shift for yourself.

64

Yes. And already the hall has cornered him again.

Shifting like this, shuffling foot by clumsy foot,
I do and undo for myself. But for you, too,
and for Scott, and the Omaha girl. Think of this
as a charm for venturers along any patient way.
May grace be drawn to our ill-suited hands.

Sundowner

"What is man but his emotional life?"
Lawrence Knopp, MD

Sundowner. There's another name, but I don't know it.
The lady in 519 D knows where she is: home.
And she wants the strangers out, like mildewed furniture,
like a sickness smell so bad the windows won't open
wide enough.

Where does such strength come from?
I could put my hand twice around the bones of her wrist.

Help, she cries, and the small nurse cries, *Help*,
mirrored claims competing like everything here,
living and dying, illness and health.

Deceitful as natural daughters, they surround her,
show her the numbers on her door. *Cunts*, she says.
Fucking bitches. She has kept these words all her days,
like bits of twine, a gun under the mattress, in case of need.

Now they herd her, like elephants protecting a newborn,
to the wide windows. See? There is the Space Needle,
the skyline spelling Seattle. And the lovely Sound,
where already in places the salmon wash up tumorous.

And there, where the sun goes down, are the Olympics,
those white clean lobes, speech and spatial relations,
left hand and right, and voices of the gods.

Around me in the corridor, patients wheel, soundless
as ghosts, or lurch like melancholy drunks.

I want it so much then I almost see it.
The sunny kitchen, that lilac blossoming wide
beyond the yellow curtains. But it's wrong,
the flaw in any poem, soft mutant stanza.
Never the surgeon, I cut nothing out.

Now it is over. They are putting her down
one more night. There is such color in her cheeks,
like a girl's after dancing.

                        I think how the sun moves
every day across our plumed, imperfect skies,
and never moves. And of this woman, traveler
all her life, caught in this white network,
home, among strangers moved no nearer her
than you or I.

Semi-Private

is semi-tough, the way footballers say, the white Texans,
huge Christian Fellows, their Christ runty enough,
you know, to specialize, that Field Goal Kicker
in tough crosswinds, nailing down the big one.

Never a cribbage player, I'm not what anyone
would choose to halve this room. Still,
stroke and counterstroke, left side and right,
two semi-ones, we make some pair.

                              Private men,
how the prefix impedes us, like a truck, an 18-wheeler,
on a narrowing road, the long haul uphill.

More than this room, we share odors, mortifications,
flowers, the public company of wishers-well.
We share one window, Seattle lifting beyond us
its great blocks, brick, cement, tile and glass.

We share the bird, a solitary gull, that arrives,
unbrooding, daily, always in its own sweet time.
Ad hoc committee, we take into our considerations
this seabird, also the laborless flowering cherries
clothed like nothing else down all the busy streets.

Shaving, we share the solemn mirror. In mid-scrape,
he falls, this time no stroke of unluck. Layman
and layman, we put him on his own stressed feet.

We are slow studies in this learned profession:
together we are stronger, and not much less wise.

When I move out, I leave him semi-fixed for life;
in return, he lives with me in style, semi-private,
crimped, not what any one of us would choose.

On First Looking Into Norton's Anthology
of Poetry (Revised)

> "Once again (I never cease to be
> amazed) you have provided an
> excellent anthology at a surprisingly
> low price. It has your usually fine but
> unobtrusive notes, and the margins
> are ample for easy reading and
> personal notation."
>
> Elton D. Higgs,
> University of Michigan, Dearborn

Collared and pulleyed by affliction, (never ceasing
to be amazed), restless again before examinations,
I am scanning George Herbert at four in the morning.
1593–1633, surprisingly low, dirt cheap and priceless.

My bag, always papery and wet, has been the moderns,
loving best those nearest my own sweet self.
Tonight, a dark one, subtracting years, I find G.H.
contemporary, and make this unobtrusive note.

Let younger poets, Iowa or Yale, giving easy readings,
ample in their margins, all those who work to shop,
learn "The Forerunners" by heart: *The harbingers
are come. See, see their mark: / White is their color,*

and behold my head. / But must they have my brain?
As a personal notation, perhaps they must.
At best, it must be scanned and dyed and marked,
brain trusted, and stormed, and one day less.

George Herbert, dearborn as E. D. Higgs, or you,
or I, has fifteen pages still, two dozen poems.
Poems a penny each, the flap puff says.
Pleasing God, says Herbert, *I write fine and witty.*

And, by God, between us, we have passed the night.
I fear for old George, his dated, rhyming dust,
squashed down by Norton's widening rear,
by Bakara, Koch, and Bly, and Don L. Lee,

and by MacBeth, a different, indifferent George,
born 1932, who writes on fourteen ways to touch
the peter. Even for a minor poet, that isn't much.
O, I know a poetess, unanthologized, ingenious . . .

This much from Seattle, 1981; the rest is England, 1633:
   Go, birds of spring, let winter have his fee;
    Let a bleak paleness chalk the door,
  So all within be livelier than before.

Comeback

April 23.

        Three months today, and I am coming back,
stepping into the Intramural Building like a man
dipping a cautious toe twice in the old same river.

Lord, what need we have of permanence! That's the one poem,
the fiction that makes nothing happen, except our lives.

No country for old men, that sweet indelible land
of lockers, the young into one another's mirrored arms,
a fishy air moist and alive as any crowded sea.

Therefore I check out a ball, count stairs, and come
to the gym where this morning there is nothing
under all these boards and netted goals but me.

This is the court where the verdict came down,
a lawful seizure, a sentence like a blow to the head.
And here, unmarked, is the space where I lay,
jerking like a mackerel in air, hooked on lines
corny as a Republican President's, living
in old movies to the happy end.

                  Now, puff-faced
and atrophied, hairless, tattooed like a death camp
Jew, I have lost some appeal. Still, it is April,
and I am here, asking nothing of nothing.

What I want, I make myself.

Over here is the spot
where I was deadly once, my seventeen-foot jumper
automatic as health, zoned or manned, double-team
or none. Today it is none.

So my left hand,
out of nature, not in golden form, bounces the ball
and it comes back, rhythmic as a sack of rocks.

Who would pass to no one with the game on the line?
I go up in sections like some whooping crane,
left leg snared, right side winging for the sky,
making myself rise.

God bless my right hand,
which forgets nothing! The ball turns on itself,
another stellar body, finds the rim, that O
of painted orange lips, escapes out the netting
one more time.

Nothing applauds. I look around.
Light is everywhere on empty boards. It is all
the past, the passing, or to come. Yes. But this,
this making, too, basket, or love, or joyful noise.
Or else some timeless athlete's self to hang in air
so fiery and refined he never hears behind him,
coming back, the sound of no hands as they clap.

Homecoming

for Marlene

After the scanning, CAT scan and radium, the arterioscan,
those warm coals flaming behind each.dumbfounded eye,
we have come home.

> After the palm readings, after
the foot scratching, after the knee jerking
and the rubber hammer, we have come home.

And after the late news, as if some baffled anchor man
threw up his hands, not sad, not happy, saying only
Everything is changed. And that's how it is.

Now, between us, we have climbed the 38 stairs,
missing none, and I am tired, remembering once
after football, twenty years ago, being tired,
worn down by little Saint Lawrence in windy Canton,
the score 22-22 forever, not knowing what to feel.

And you have homecoming gifts, a plastic ring
for pills, each day of the week in script,
like a stewardess's underwear. That, and our own
high window where you give your hand to mine,
this left one, where nothing else holds right.

And see! The lights of Ballard, clusters
and nebulae, lovely tonight as any galaxy
beneath the great horned toe of God.

74

Holding on like this, finding my grip,
we are naming the constellations one by one:
Market Street and the bridge and the locks
where, last summer, the salmon leaped for us.
Holding and naming, we are healing each other.

And beyond Ballard, the end of the earth,
miles out on the black of Puget Sound,
two boats, no more lost than all the planets,
bear their small lights outward, to the sea.

Colophon

Among those whose efforts have aided in the production of this volume are Irish Setter (Portland, Oregon), who set the Bembo type; Thomson-Shore, Inc. (Dexter, Michigan), manufacturers; G. Scott Freutel of Spring Valley Press (Langley, Washington), who designed and set type for the cover; Tim Hall, calligrapher; and Kim Stafford, production manager.